Nita Mehta's
Thai
cooking

Nita Mehta

B.Sc. (Home Science), M.Sc. (Food and Nutrition), Gold Medalist

Nita Mehta's
Thai
cooking

ISBN 81-7869-125-6

Exclusive Distributor:

AM PRODUCTIONS
DIVISION OF: INFORMATION SCIENCE INDUSTRIES (CANADA) LIMITED

1169 Parisien St., Ottawa, Ont., K1B 4W4,
Tel: 613.745.3098 Fax: 613.745.7533
e-mail: amproductions@rogers.com
web: www.amproductions.ca

Published by:

SNAB
Publishers Pvt. Ltd.
3A/3 Asaf Ali Road,
New Delhi - 110002
Tel: 23252948, 23250091
Telefax: 91-11-23250091
INDIA

Editorial and Marketing office:
E-159, Greater Kailash-II, N.Delhi-48
Fax: 91-11-29225218, 29229558
Tel: 91-11-29214011, 29218727, 29218574
E-Mail: nitamehta@email.com, nitamehta@nitamehta.com
Website: http://www.nitamehta.com
Website: http://www.snabindia.com

Printed at:

BRIJBASI ART PRESS LIMITED

Price: $ 5.95

Contents

soups & salads   15

main course   31

snacks & dips   21

noodles & rice   41

desserts   46

Introduction

For the lighthearted people of Thailand, food is a celebration. The brilliant colours, delicious aromas and exotic spices are designed to lift the spirit. At the same time, the style of cooking is fast, fresh and healthy, making it ideal for today's world.

The tapestry of Thai Cuisine is richly woven with threads from China and India. From China they learnt the art of stir-frying and steaming and whole-heartedly adopted their love of noodles. Instead of soya sauce, they chose fish sauce and substituted the sourness of vinegar with their own fragrant limes and lemons. India has given them spices like coriander and cumin, taken straight out of the Indian spice-box and stirred into their famous red, green and yellow curry pastes.

The illustrations in this book, along with the straightforward instructions, will help and inspire you to make well-known dishes like Tom Yum Soup and Pad Thai, as well as the traditional Chicken in Red Curry with Mushrooms, Crispy Vegetables, with Date Pancakes for dessert. Discover the excitement of cooking classic Thai meals in your own home!

Nita Mehta

INTERNATIONAL CONVERSION GUIDE

These are not exact equivalents; they've been rounded-off to make measuring easier.

WEIGHTS & MEASURES

METRIC	IMPERIAL
15 g	½ oz
30 g	1 oz
60 g	2 oz
90 g	3 oz
125 g	4 oz (¼ lb)
155 g	5 oz
185 g	6 oz
220 g	7 oz
250 g	8 oz (½ lb)
280 g	9 oz
315 g	10 oz
345 g	11 oz
375 g	12 oz (¾ lb)
410 g	13 oz
440 g	14 oz
470 g	15 oz
500 g	16 oz (1 lb)
750 g	24 oz (1½ lb)
1 kg	30 oz (2 lb)

LIQUID MEASURES

METRIC	IMPERIAL
30 ml	1 fluid oz
60 ml	2 fluid oz
100 ml	3 fluid oz
125 ml	4 fluid oz
150 ml	5 fluid oz (¼ pint/1 gill)
190 ml	6 fluid oz
250 ml	8 fluid oz
300 ml	10 fluid oz (½ pint)
500 ml	16 fluid oz
600 ml	20 fluid oz (1 pint)
1000 ml	1¾ pints

CUPS & SPOON MEASURES

METRIC	IMPERIAL
1 ml	¼ tsp
2 ml	½ tsp
5 ml	1 tsp
15 ml	1 tbsp
60 ml	¼ cup
125 ml	½ cup
250 ml	1 cup

HELPFUL MEASURES

METRIC	IMPERIAL
3 mm	1/8 in
6 mm	¼ in
1 cm	½ in
2 cm	¾ in
2.5 cm	1 in
5 cm	2 in
6 cm	2½ in
8 cm	3 in
10 cm	4 in
13 cm	5 in
15 cm	6 in
18 cm	7 in
20 cm	8 in
23 cm	9 in
25 cm	10 in
28 cm	11 in
30 cm	12 in (1ft)

HOW TO MEASURE

When using the graduated metric measuring cups, it is important to shake the dry ingredients loosely into the required cup. Do not tap the cup on the table, or pack the ingredients into the cup unless otherwise directed. Level top of cup with a knife. When using graduated metric measuring spoons, level top of spoon with a knife. When measuring liquids in the jug, place jug on a flat surface, check for accuracy at eye level.

OVEN TEMPERATURE

These oven temperatures are only a guide. Always check the manufacturer's manual.

	°C (Celsius)	°F (Fahrenheit)	Gas Mark
Very low	120	250	1
Low	150	300	2
Moderately low	160	325	3
Moderate	180	350	4
Moderately high	190	375	5
High	200	400	6
Very high	230	450	7

Ingredients used in Thai food

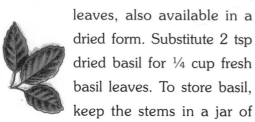

Basil: A fragrant herb with fresh green leaves, also available in a dried form. Substitute 2 tsp dried basil for ¼ cup fresh basil leaves. To store basil, keep the stems in a jar of water, the leaves above the level of the water – this keeps them fresh and green for a few days. In winter leave the jar at room temperature. In summer keep the jar in the fridge.

Lemon Grass: A long flavourful stalk, with the upper portion resembling grass. Only the stalk is edible since the grassy part is very chewy. The flavour of lemon grass is similar to that of lemon, yet it has its very own unique taste. To use, discard the bottom ½" of the stalk and peel some

of the outer leaves. Chop the stalk and use it in curry pastes. The upper grass-like portion is not edible, so it is added to dishes like soups, rice and curries to flavour them but removed from the dish before serving. Lemon grass will keep well for about 1-2 weeks in the fridge. Use 1-2 stalks per dish. In the absence of lemon grass, use lemon rind.

Lemon Rind: To get lemon rind, grate a firm fresh lemon on the fine holes of the grater without applying pressure. Grate only the yellow outer skin without grating the white pith beneath it. Rind of 1 lemon gives as much flavour as 1 stalk of lemon grass.

In the absence of lemon grass, lemon rind is a good substitute.

Black Bean Sauce: This sauce is made from fermented black beans. It has a pungent and salty flavour. It cannot be made at home. It is available ready-made in bottles, at most leading grocery stores.

Soup Cube & Stock: Stock is the base for soups and sauces. However, if you do not have stock ready or feel lazy to make a stock, you can use soup cubes mixed in water instead. These cubes are available as small packets. They make the food salty, so taste the dish before you put in more salt. Always crush the soup cube to a powder before using it.

Five Spice Powder: This ground mixture of five spices is slightly sweet and pungent. Roast together 2 tsp peppercorns, 3 star anise, 6 cloves, 4" stick cinnamon and 3 tsp fennel. Grind all the ingredients in a small mixer to make a powder. Sift through a sieve to get a fine powder.

Soya Sauce: This sauce is made from fermented soya beans. It is very salty and adds a distinct flavour and colour to the dish. There are 2 kinds: one is dark and the other is light. Both are used for seasoning foods. The sauce gets concentrated if stored for a long time so if you have an old bottle lying around, use less than the quantity mentioned in the recipes.

Fish Sauce: This is a thin, very light brown sauce. It is a fermented sauce made from fish packed in wooden barrels. It is salty in taste and has a distinct flavour of its own. It is available ready-made in bottles like soya sauce. Soya sauce makes a good substitute for fish sauce for vegetarian cooking.

Kaffir Lime Leaves: These have a distinctive flavour and perfume. The leaves are available dried, frozen or fresh. The fresh leaves are used whole or can be shredded before adding to the food. When

shredding, discard the thick centre vein. If kaffir lime leaves are unavailable, any leaves of a lemon plant would work. In this book we have not specified the use of kaffir limes for lime juice, but for a true Thai flavour, use it whenever possible.

Coconut Cream and Milk: This liquid is extracted from coconut flesh. Coconut cream is the liquid extracted from the first pressing of coconuts. Coconut cream is the thickest and most concentrated extract. Coconut milk is the product of the second and third pressing and is much thinner. Coconut milk is used in curries, while coconut cream is used mainly in desserts. Coconut cream is available in tetra packs or cans and can be diluted with water to make coconut milk. Coconut milk powder is also available which can be mixed with some water to make coconut milk.

Star Anise : The dried, hard, brown, star-shaped fruit has the flavour of fennel. It is an important ingredient in five-spice powder. It can be substituted

with fennel, if unavailable. Can be used whole or in a ground form.

Noodles: Thin noodles are preferred to thick ones. They are usually cooked in boiling water till just done for about 1 minute only. Never overcook noodles as they turn thick if overcooked. They are cooked to the al' dente stage (see p 48).

Rice Noodles: Rice noodles can be in the form of flat, thick sticks or very fine threads. These thin noodles resemble long, translucent white hair and are called rice vermicelli also. Rice noodles are just soaked in hot water for about 5-10 minutes, depending on the thickness of the noodles. Cover them when they are being soaked so that the water remains

hot. Drain and rinse for use. Sometimes, for garnish, thin rice noodles are deep fried when they explode dramatically into a tangle of airy, crunchy strands.

White Glutinous Rice/Sticky Rice: This rice can either be long or short-grained for savoury dishes, Thai cooks would use the long-grain variety. Glutinous rice is very high in starch content, the cooked grains cling together in a mass and are soft and sticky. Short- grain white glutinous rice is mainly used for desserts.

Rice Flour: This is raw rice ground to a powder. The addition of rice flour to batters makes the food crisp. To make it at home, grind raw rice to a smooth powder. Sift through a sieve to get a fine powder.

Bean Sprouts: These are shoots of moong beans or soya beans. The texture is crisp. To make bean sprouts at home, soak ½ cup of green moong beans for about 8 hours. Discard water & tie in a muslin cloth. Keep it tied for 2-3 days, remembering to wet the cloth each day. When shoots are long enough, wash carefully in water. Fresh bean sprouts will keep for 3-4 days if refrigerated in a plastic bag.

Bean Curd/Tofu: This is fresh cheese made by curdling soya bean milk. The firm tofu can be pan fried too where as the soft, silken tofu is only suitable for fillings and salads. It resembles Indian paneer (cheese made by curdling cow's milk) in taste and appearance.

Dry Red Chilli: These are easily available in markets. They are really hot. You can deseed them to decrease their heat. The thinner variety is hotter than the thick ones. They are usually soaked and ground to a paste in the curries.

Shallots: These belongs to the onion family but are smaller in size and milder in flavour.

Ginger/Galangal: Galangal is the Thai ginger, which has a mild flavour. The Thais use a wide variety of different 'gingers' in their cooking, all of which have subtle differences. If all the varieties are not available, use regular ginger instead.

Choose a very young or fresh ginger as it has a milder flavour. A good indication of young ginger is that the skin should be thin, soft and pale in colour.

Simple Thai Garnishes

MANGO HEDGEHOG:

Take a small ripe, firm mango, avoid using the fibrous variety. Slice off two pieces from either side of the seed. Cut parallel lines with a knife, about ½" apart, along the length of the mango. Cut parallel lines at right angles to these, the same distance apart. You must go right down to the skin, but be extremely careful that you do not cut through the skin. Hold slice firmly & with the tips of your fingers, push it out from the back, carefully, applying pressure on the thickest part. The slice will open out to resemble a hedgehog, and will retain this shape. Use this as a garnish to decorate desserts & cakes. You can do the same with plums, kiwi etc.

CARROT & RADISH TUBEROSE:

Take a slender carrot or radish. Peel and wash it. Make a sharp angled cut, at about a height of 1½", about ½" downwards and inwards. Make 2 similar cuts from the remaining sides - all the cuts should meet at the end. Hold the top of the carrot with one hand, and the base with the other. Twist the lower portion to break off the top portion. You will have a tuberose in one hand and the remaining part of the carrot in the other. Trim the left over carrot to get a pointed end. Make more flowers from the left over carrot. Keep them in ice-cold water for upto 3-4 days without getting spoilt. You can make such flowers with white radish also. These look great when placed on the side of a salad, or next to the snacks on the serving platter. A sprig of green leaves of cilantro/coriander, mint or parsley placed next to the flowers make them look prettier.

BELL PEPPER BASKET:

Slice the top of a yellow, red or green bell pepper. Make ½" deep V cuts all around the edge to get a 'VVVV' edge. Insert a sprig of parsley or any greens in it. Place on the side of a large platter of salad.

CHILLI FLOWER:

Choose a slightly thick chilli. Cut into half starting from the tip almost till the end, leaving ½" from the stem end. Cut each half with a pair of scissors into many thin strips, keeping all intact at the base. Put the chilli in chilled water for 4-5 hours in the fridge. It opens up to a flower. A chilli flower made from fresh red or green chilli is a wonderful garnish for a spicy dish.

GREEN ONION FLOWER:

To make a green onion flower, cut off about ¼ inch piece from the white bulb end and leaving 3" from the bulb, cut off the greens. Slice the bulb thinly lengthwise till the end of the bulb. Now make similar cuts at right angles. Similarly for a green side, cut the green leaves with a pair of scissors, almost till the end to get thin strips. Place in iced water for some time until it opens up like a flower.

Mango Hedge Hog

Carrot & Radish Tuberose

Bell pepper Basket

Chilli Flower

Green Onion Flower

CURRY PASTES

You can make these curry pastes well in advance and freeze them for a month.

Red Curry Paste

No green ingredients like basil or lemon leaves are added in the paste as this discolours the red colour of the paste.

Serves 4

INGREDIENTS

4-5 dry, red chillies, (preferably the broad variety as it imparts a bright red colour)
½ onion - chopped
8 flakes garlic - peeled & chopped (1 tbsp)
½" piece galangal/ginger - chopped (1 tsp)
1 stick lemon grass (use only the lower portion, discard the leaves) - cut into small pieces or rind of 1 lemon (see p. 6)
½ tsp peppercorns (*saboot kali mirch*)
1 tsp salt, ¼ tsp turmeric (*haldi*)
1 tbsp coriander seeds (*saboot dhania*)
1 tsp cumin seeds *(jeera)*
1 tbsp lemon juice

METHOD

1 Break the red chillies into two pieces and discard seeds; soak in ¼ cup warm water for 10 minutes.

2 In a skillet, dry-roast cumin and coriander seeds on low heat for about 2 minutes till they turn fragrant and get roasted but not brown.

3 Put the red chillies, along with their soaking water, into a grinder. Add the roasted seeds and all the remaining ingredients. Grind to a smooth paste. Use as required.

Green Curry Paste

Green ingredients like basil and lemon leaves are added in the paste to enhance the colour and taste of the green paste.

Serves 4

INGREDIENTS

6-7 green chillies
1 cup fresh basil leaves or ½ cup chopped cilantro leaves and stems (*hara dhaniya*)
2-3 lemon leaves (*nimbu ke patte*)
½ onion - chopped
1 tbsp chopped garlic
½" piece ginger - chopped (1 tsp)
1 stick lemon grass (use only the lower portion, discard the leaves) - cut into small pieces or rind of 1 lemon (see p. 6)
½ tsp salt
1 tsp peppercorns (*saboot kali mirch*)
1 tbsp lemon juice
1 tbsp coriander seeds (*saboot dhania*)
1 tsp cumin seeds (*jeera*)

METHOD

1 Deseed green chillies and chop them.

2 In a skillet, dry roast cumin and coriander seeds on low heat for about 2 minutes till they become fragrant & roasted but not browned.

3 Put all the ingredients of the curry paste and the roasted seeds in a grinder and grind to a fine paste, using a little water for grinding. Use as required.

Yellow Curry Paste

Serves 4

INGREDIENTS

3 tbsp chopped, fresh yellow or
red chillies or 6 dried red chillies
1 stick lemon grass (use only the lower
portion, discard the leaves) - cut into small
pieces or rind of 1 lemon (see p. 6)
½ onion - finely chopped
1 tbsp chopped garlic
½" piece ginger or galangal - thinly sliced
1 tbsp lemon juice
1 tsp salt
3 tsp turmeric powder (*haldi*)

SPICES - ROAST TOGETHER
1½ tsp coriander seeds (*dhania saboot*)
¼ tsp peppercorns (*saboot kali mirch*)
1 star anise (*phool chakri*) or
1 tsp fennel seeds (*saunf*)
2 cloves (*laung*)
1" stick cinnamon (*dalchini*)

METHOD

1 Put all the spices in a skillet and dry roast for about 2-3 minutes on low heat, till fragrant. Let them cool. Crush roughly.

2 Put all the ingredients in a grinder. Add the roasted and crushed spices. Grind to a paste, using a little water. Use as required.

Masaman Curry Paste

A spicy strong-flavoured paste.

Serves 4

INGREDIENTS

2 onions - chopped (1 cup)
1½ tbsp chopped garlic
1½ tbsp chopped ginger
rind of 1 lemon (see p. 6)
¼ tsp grated nutmeg (*jaiphal*)

SPICES - ROAST TOGETHER
10 dried, red chillies - deseeded
2 tbsp cumin seeds (*jeera*)
2 tsp fennel seeds (*saunf*)
2" stick cinnamon (*dalchini*)
seeds of 4 brown cardamoms (*moti elaichi*)
4 cloves (*laung*)
8 black peppercorns (*saboot kali mirch*)
4 tbsp coriander seeds (*saboot dhania*)

METHOD

1 Roast all spices in a skillet for 3-4 minutes or till fragrant.

2 Put all other ingredients in a mixer. Add the roasted spices. Grind all to a paste with a little water. Use as required.

Soups
&
Salads

Green Mango-Cashew Salad

A very unusual quick salad made with green mangoes. It is flavoured with ready-made mango chutney but if this is not available, plum, date or tamarind conserve may be used instead.

Serves 6-8

INGREDIENTS

3 cups juliennes (match sticks) of raw green, mangoes (about 3 mangoes)
½ cup roasted cashews
1-2 green onions *(hara pyaz)*
2 tbsp ready-made mango chutney
1-2 dry red chillies - crushed (½ tsp)
1-2 tsp soya sauce
salt and pepper to taste
1 tsp crushed garlic
1 tsp honey or powdered sugar if needed
½ tsp ground cumin *(jeera powder)*

METHOD

1. Cut the white bulb of green onions into rings and the greens into 1" diagonal pieces.

2. Peel green mangoes. Cut the side pieces. Cut into thin match sticks or juliennes.

3. Mix all ingredients except cashew nuts and honey in a bowl. If mangoes are very sour add honey or sugar. Keep covered in the refrigerator for 2 hours for the flavours to infuse.

4. At serving time, top with roasted nuts and mix lightly.

Tom Yum Soup

A thin, spicy soup with vegetables floating on top. The vegetables need to be cut as thinly as possible, or they will all sink to the bottom.

Serves 4

INGREDIENTS

1-2 mushrooms - cut into paper thin slices
½ small carrot - cut into paper-thin diagonal slices
¼ cup of very tiny pieces of broccoli without stem
2 fresh red or green chillies - sliced diagonally and deseeded
1 tbsp whole cilantro/coriander leaves
2-3 tbsp lemon juice
2 tsp sugar
5 cups stock or 5 cups water mixed with 2 stock or soup cubes
1-2 tsp light soya sauce or fish sauce
¾ tsp salt & ¼ tsp pepper, or to taste
1 tbsp oil
3-4 kaffir lime leaves/lemon leaves - shredded
½ stalk lemon grass - cut into very thin slices diagonally

PASTE (CRUSH TOGETHER)
½ tsp red chilli flakes
2-3 flakes garlic, ½ tsp chopped ginger
½ tsp salt

METHOD

1 In a deep pan heat 1 tbsp oil, add lemon leaves and lemon grass and the above paste. Stir for a minute on medium heat.

2 Add stock or water mixed with soup cubes. Give one boil. Reduce heat and keep covered on low heat for 5 minutes.

3 Add mushrooms, carrots, broccoli and fresh red chillies. Boil for 2 minutes.

4 Reduce heat. Add lemon juice, light soya sauce, salt, pepper and sugar to taste. Add cilantro/coriander leaves. Simmer for 1 minute.

5 Remove from heat. Serve hot in soup bowls.

Thai Egg Salad

Serves 4

INGREDIENTS

3 hard-boiled eggs
½ cup coarsely chopped green (raw)
mango or a cooking apple
¼ cup mint leaves *(pudina)*
2 tbsp chopped onions, preferably green
onions
½ cup shredded cabbage
½ cup grated carrot

DRESSING
3 tbsp lemon juice
1 green chilli - sliced
2 tbsp chopped garlic
1 tsp salt
2 tbsp salad oil or any cooking oil

GARNISH
lettuce leaves and tomato wedges

METHOD

1. Grind together for the dressing — lemon juice, green chilli, garlic, salt and oil. Keep aside.

2. Peel and cut the boiled eggs into ½" thick slices or ½" pieces. Keep aside.

3. Mix together all the other ingredients. Pour most of the dressing on top. Mix well.

4. Add the boiled eggs and pour the remaining dressing on the eggs. Toss lightly.

5. Garnish with lettuce leaves and tomato wedges.

Note: *To hard boil an egg, boil the egg in water for 8 minutes. Remove from water and immediately put in cold water. Immersing the boiled egg in cold water, prevents the formation of a black ring around the yolk.*

Shrimp (Prawn) Soup

Serves 4

INGREDIENTS

250 g/8 oz uncooked small shrimps
(prawns)
4½ cups water
4-5 whole lime leaves
1 tbsp chopped lemon grass
1 tsp fish sauce
2 tbsp chopped cilantro/coriander leaves
1½ tbsp sliced green onions
1 red chilli - deseeded and sliced into
1 inch strips
2 tbsp fresh lemon juice
salt and pepper to taste

METHOD

1 To prepare the shrimps/prawns, shell them and remove the dark vein running along the back. Wash them under running water, drain and pat dry with absorbent kitchen paper. Set aside while you make the soup.

2 Pour the water into a large saucepan and bring to a boil. Add the lime leaves and chopped lemon grass, reduce the heat and simmer for 10 minutes.

3 Add the fish sauce and cook for further 5 minutes.

4 Add the shrimps/prawns and lime juice to the pan and cook gently over very low heat for 2-3 minutes, until the shrimps/prawns become firm and turn a pale pink colour.

5 Add the chopped cilantro/coriander leaves, green onions and red chilli strips to the soup.

6 Add the seasonings - salt, pepper and lemon juice, making it really piquant, and serve very hot in small bowls.

Snacks & Dips

Spring Rolls

Thai spring rolls are usually served whole without cutting them into smaller pieces. So it is good to roll out small wrappers for them.

Makes 10-12

INGREDIENTS

WRAPPER
¾ cup plain flour (*maida*)
½ cup cornstarch
1 tsp salt, 1 tbsp oil
oil for frying

FILLING
1 cup shredded green cabbage
½ cup shredded red cabbage
½ cup grated carrots
½ cup shredded green bell pepper
100 g/4 oz tofu - cut into ½" pieces, deep fried till golden
1 tbsp oil
½ tsp crushed garlic
½ onion - cut into slices widthwise
1 tbsp soya sauce, 1 tbsp lemon juice
¼ cup basil leaves - shredded
¼ tsp red chilli flakes or powder
½ tsp sugar
½ tsp salt & pepper, or to taste
3 tbsp roasted peanuts - crushed roughly

SEALING PASTE
1 tbsp cornstarch mixed with 1 tbsp water

METHOD

1 To prepare the wrappers, sift plain flour, cornstarch and salt. Add water gradually, mixing to make a very stiff dough. Add oil and knead very well till very smooth and elastic. Cover with a damp cloth and keep aside for ½ hour.

2 Make small balls from the dough. Roll into thin chappatis of 5 inch diameter. Heat a griddle & put one thinly rolled chappati on it. Cook on both sides for 2-3 seconds. Keep covered in a damp cloth in a box.

3 To make filling, heat 1 tbsp oil and add onion and garlic. Stir for a minute. Add both the cabbage, carrot & green bell pepper. Give a quick stir.

4 Add fried tofu, soya sauce, lemon juice, basil, red chilli powder or flakes, sugar, pepper and salt. Mix well. Add crushed peanuts, mix well. Remove from heat. Check seasonings. Let it cool. Crumble the tofu lightly.

5 To assemble the wrapper, spread a chappati on a flat surface.

6 Spread some filling thinly, leaving 1" from the front edge.

7 Fold ½" from the right & the left side.

8 Hold the folds in place and roll to cover the filling. Move forward to get a spring roll, making sure that all the filling is enclosed.

9 Seal edges with cornstarch paste. If you chill the rolls for ½ hour, they keep in better shape. Keep aside till serving time.

10 Heat some oil in a large frying pan. Reduce heat and put the rolls, seam-side down in oil. Cook on all sides until crisp and golden. Drain on absorbent paper. Serve with sweet and sour dip given on page 24.

Fragrant Meat Balls

These tasty meat balls can be made from minced lamb, pork or chicken.

Makes 24-25 balls

INGREDIENTS

MEAT BALLS
500 g/1 lb ground meat or mince
1 tbsp chopped garlic
4-5 green onions - finely chopped or 2
onions - chopped (1 cup)
1 tbsp chopped fresh cilantro/coriander
5 tbsp red curry paste (see p. 12)
1 tbsp lemon juice
1 tbsp fish sauce (optional)
1 tsp salt, or to taste, ½ tsp pepper
1 egg

OTHER INGREDIENTS
rice flour for coating, see note
oil for deep frying
sprigs of cilantro/coriander for garnishing

METHOD

1 Wash mince in a strainer. Squeeze out all the water.

2 Put mince and all other ingredients for the meat balls in the mixer. Blend in the mixer for a few seconds to mix well.

3 Make balls, roll in rice flour. Dust off the excess. Deep-fry all together on low heat till golden and the mince gets cooked. Serve hot, garnished with cilantro/coriander.

Note: *Instead of rice flour, dry bread crumbs can be used for coating meatballs.*

Sweet and Sour Dip

Serve this sweet and tangy dip with any deep-fried starter.

Makes ½ cup (approx.)

INGREDIENTS

a lemon sized ball of tamarind (*imli*)
or 1 tbsp ready made tamarind pulp
¼ cup jaggery (*gur*), ½ tsp lemon juice
½ tsp salt, ¼ tsp red chilli powder

METHOD

1 Boil ¼ cup water and tamarind in a pan. Give one boil. Remove from heat. Strain through a sieve, mashing with the back of a spoon to get pulp. You can also use ready-made tamarind pulp.

2 In another pan put 1 tbsp of tamarind pulp, jaggery, salt, red chilli powder and ¼ cup water. Give one boil. Remove from heat. Add lemon juice. Check seasonings. Chill and serve.

Vegetable Dim Sums

These delicious snacks are steamed in a steamer basket & served with a dipping sauce.

Makes 14 pieces

INGREDIENTS

DOUGH
1 cup flour *(maida)*, ¼ tsp salt, 1 tbsp oil

FILLING
2 tbsp oil
1 onion - finely chopped
4-5 mushrooms - finely chopped, optional
1 large carrot - grated
2 green chillies - finely chopped
1 tsp ginger-garlic paste
2 cups grated cauliflower or cabbage
1 tsp salt & ½ tsp pepper powder
or to taste
1 tsp lemon juice

DIPPING SAUCE
4-5 tbsp Soya sauce
2 tbsp white vinegar, 1- 2 tbsp oil
4 flakes garlic - crushed to a paste
½ tsp red chilli powder, ¼ tsp salt
1 tbsp tomato ketchup

METHOD

1   For the dough, sift flour with salt. Add oil and knead with enough water to make a stiff dough of rolling consistency. Knead till very smooth. Cover with a damp cloth and keep aside.

2   For the filling, heat oil. Add chopped onion. Fry till soft. Add mushrooms, cook further for 2-3 minutes. Add cauliflower or cabbage and ginger-garlic paste, cook for 2 minutes. Add carrot and green chillies. Mix well. Stir-fry on high heat for 1 minute. Add salt, pepper to taste. Add lemon juice and mix well. Remove from heat and keep filling aside.

3   Take out the dough and form small balls. Roll out as thin as possible into small rounds of 2½ inch diameter.

4   Put some stuffing in the centre and close into a ball. Roll the ball between the hands to give it an elongated shape like a roll.

5   To steam, put them in a steamer and steam for 10 minutes.

6   Cool the dimsums. Cut a slice from the top to expose the filling. Dot with chilli sauce.

7   For dipping sauce, mix all ingredients in a bowl. Serve with dimsums.

Satay with Peanut Sauce

This chicken-on-skewers is delicious but for a chage use 400 g/12 oz of button mushrooms instead.

Serves 6

INGREDIENTS

400 g/12 oz chicken - boneless bite-size pieces
6 bamboo skewers - soaked in water to prevent burning

MARINADE

2 tsp oil, 1 tbsp soya sauce
1" piece of ginger - grated
1 tbsp lemon juice, 1 tbsp cornstarch
8-10 flakes garlic - crushed (1½ tsp)
1½ tsp ground cumin (*jeera powder*)
1½ tsp ground coriander (*dhania powder*)
¾ tsp red chilli powder
2 tsp brown sugar or *gur*, ½ tsp salt
2 fresh red chillies - deseeded & sliced
3 tbsp coconut milk or coconut milk powder (Maggi) mixed with 2 tbsp milk

PEANUT SAUCE

¼ cup roasted salted peanuts, ½ tsp salt
2 tbsp oil, ½ onion - chopped
½ tsp red chilli powder, ½-1 tsp sugar
1 tsp ground coriander (*dhania powder*)
1 tsp ground cumin (*jeera powder*)
4-6 flakes garlic - crushed (1 tsp)
1½ tsp lemon juice, 1 tsp soya sauce
¾-1 cup ready-made coconut milk

METHOD

1 Mix all the marinade ingredients thoroughly in a bowl.

2 Add chicken pieces to the marinade, mix very well. Leave aside for at least 2 hours or overnight in the refrigerator.

3 Thread marinated chicken pieces onto wooden skewers. Do not leave any space between each piece while threading them. Leave behind the marinade.

4 Cook in a preheated oven at 220°C for 10-12 minutes, turning them once in between & basting with the remaining marinade. Alternately, heat a non-stick skillet, grease it slightly with a few drops of oil & place skewered chicken, a few at a time. Cook on medium heat, turning them frequently. Cook till chicken turns tender and golden brown.

5 To make peanut sauce, grind peanuts with the salt to a rough powder.

6 Heat 2 tbsp oil in a heavy-based small pan. Add crushed garlic. Saute till it starts to change colour. Add onion and cook till soft. Reduce heat. Add red chilli powder, ground coriander and cumin. Add only ½ cup coconut milk. Boil, stirring. Cook on low heat for 3 minutes, stirring constantly.

7 Add crushed peanuts, sugar, lemon juice, Soya sauce and the remaining ½ cup coconut milk. Boil. Simmer gently for 5 minutes, stirring occasionally to prevent it from sticking to the pan. Check seasonings. Serve sauce with satay.

Fish Cakes with Pickled Cucumber

These wonderful fish cakes are a familiar and a very popular appetizer of Thailand.

Makes 12-14 cakes (patties)

INGREDIENTS

300 g/10 oz fish - cut into small pieces,
boneless and preferably skinless
2-3 lemon leaves, whole
¼ tsp ground star anise
¼ tsp ground cinnamon (*dalchini*)
5-6 tbsp red curry paste (see p. 12)
or 2 tsp red chilli paste
1 egg
50 g/2 oz green beans - chopped very
finely, 6 tbsp cornstarch
2 tbsp fish sauce
2-3 big flakes of garlic - chopped (1 tbsp)
1 tsp salt, ½ tsp sugar/jaggery
3 lemon leaves - shredded
2 tbsp chopped cilantro/coriander leaves

PICKLED CUCUMBER
4 tbsp vinegar, 4 tbsp water
2 tbsp sugar, 1 tsp salt
2-3 flakes garlic paste or minced
1 small cucumber - cut into thin slices
1 small onion - finely sliced
1 tbsp ginger juliennes
2 green/red chillies - sliced

METHOD

1 To prepare the pickled cucumber, cook together vinegar, water, sugar and salt. When sugar dissolves, give 2-3 boils and remove from heat.

2 Add the remaining ingredients and mix well. Keep aside.

3 If using fish with skin, heat a pan of water with whole lemon leaves. When it boils, add fish. Let it cook for 4-5 minutes. Remove fish from water. Now the skin can be removed very easily.

4 If using skinless fish it can be used raw and step 3 can be omitted.

5 Put fish, egg and curry paste in the mixer. Add ground star anise and cinnamon. Blend well to get a smooth mixture. Transfer to a bowl. Mix all other ingredients including beans & cornstarch. Mix well. Shape into small patties and deep fry in hot oil till golden brown.

6 Serve hot with pickled cucumber or any sauce or dip of your choice.

Note: *If patties break on frying, increase the cornstarch by 1-2 tbsp.*

Curries
&
Stir-Fries

Vegetables in Yellow Curry

Serves 4-5

INGREDIENTS

1 recipe quantity yellow curry paste (see p.14)
4 tbsp oil
1" piece of ginger peeled & sliced thinly
2 tbsp roasted peanuts (*moongphali*) - roughly crushed
2 vegetable soup cubes - crushed to a powder
2½ cups ready-made coconut milk
½-1 cup water, optional
5-6 lemon leaves (*nimbu ke patte*)
1 tbsp finely chopped lemon grass (use only stem, see note given at the end)
15 whole basil leaves or chopped cilantro
1 tsp brown sugar or regular sugar

VEGETABLES

8 medium florets of broccoli or cauliflower
100 g/4 oz babycorns - each cut into 2 pieces, lengthwise
¼ cup tinned bamboo shoots (optional)

METHOD

1   Heat 4 tbsp oil in a wok. Add yellow curry paste. Fry for 3-4 minutes on low heat.

2   Add ginger, peanuts, soup cubes & vegetables. Mix well for 2 minutes.

3   Add coconut milk, lemon leaves, chopped lemon grass, basil leaves and sugar. Give 3-4 boils. If required, add some water and cook for a few minutes. Serve hot with steamed rice or noodles.

Note: *Discard 1" from the bottom of the lemon grass. Peel a few outer leaves. Chop into ½" pieces up to the stem. Discard the upper grass like portion.*

Chicken in Red Curry with Mushrooms

Serves 4-5

INGREDIENTS

400 g/12 oz diced boneless chicken
(chicken with bones can also be used)
4 tbsp oil
1 recipe quantity red curry paste (see p.12)
4-5 lemon leaves
1 stalk lemon grass - chopped finely
3 cups coconut milk
100 g/4 oz mushrooms - sliced thickly
1 tsp salt, 1 tsp sugar and 1 tbsp lemon
juice - to blanch mushrooms
1-2 tbsp fish sauce
salt to taste, 1½ tsp sugar/jaggery
2-3 fresh green or red chillies - sliced
lengthwise
15-20 basil leaves - whole

METHOD

1 Boil 4 cups water with 1 tsp salt, 1 tsp sugar and 1 tbsp lemon juice. Add mushrooms to boiling water. Boil for 2-3 minutes till tender. Remove from water and keep blanched mushrooms aside.

2 Heat oil in a wok/pan. Add the prepared red curry paste and stir fry for 2 minutes till it smells fragrant and the oil separates.

3 Add chicken, lemon leaves and lemon grass. Fry for 3 minutes.

4 Stir in half the coconut milk. Boil. Cover, lower heat and cook till chicken is tender, about 7-8 minutes.

5 Add mushrooms, remaining coconut milk and all the remaining ingredients. Boil, simmer for 2 minutes. Check salt and adjust to taste.

6 Serve hot garnished with basil leaves.

Note: *The mushrooms taste juicy and soft if blanched before adding to the curry. Adding lemon juice to the water in which they are blanched, helps to keep them white.*

Crispy Vegetables

Serves 4

INGREDIENTS

1 cup cauliflower or broccoli florets
4 mushrooms - each cut in half
8 babycorns - keep whole
1 tbsp oil, 1 tsp garlic paste
1 onion - cut into 8 pieces
½ red bell pepper, ½ yellow bell pepper,
½ green bell pepper - cut into 1" square
20 basil leaves - keep whole, remove stem

BATTER

½ cup cornstarch
¼ cup rice flour or plain flour
1 tbsp finely chopped lemon grass
1 tsp soya sauce
1 tbsp oil
½ tsp red chilli flakes, ¾ tsp salt
½ cup chilled water- approx.

PASTE

1 tbsp lemon juice, 1 tbsp oil
4 dry, red chillies - deseeded
1 tbsp black bean sauce
3 tbsp ready-made mango chutney or date
and tamarind conserve
1 tsp soya sauce
1" stick cinnamon (*dalchini*)
1 tbsp tomato ketchup, 1 tsp honey
½ tsp salt
½ tsp cumin (*jeera*)

METHOD

1. Mix all the ingredients of the batter in a bowl, adding just enough water to get a thick pouring batter of a coating consistency. Add cauliflower, baby corns and mushrooms to the batter and keep aside for 30 minutes or more for the flavours to penetrate.

2. Mix all ingredients of the paste in a mixer and grind to a smooth paste. Keep aside.

3. Heat oil for deep frying in a wok. Mix the vegetables in the batter well and deep-fry till golden brown and crisp. To keep them crisp, keep fried vegetables in a single layer, do not heap the veggies.

4. At serving time, heat 1 tbsp oil. Add 1 tsp garlic paste and onions. Stir fry for 2 minutes. Add the bell peppers. Stir.

5. Add the paste. Stir fry for 2 minutes.

6. Add fried vegetables and basil, mix well and serve.

Tofu in Bean Sauce

Serves 4

INGREDIENTS

250 g/8 oz tofu or *paneer* - cut into
1" square pieces
100 g/ 4 oz green beans or snow peas
3 tbsp oil
2 onions - chopped very finely (1 cup)
4 flakes garlic - finely chopped (1 tsp)
1 tsp grated ginger
1 fresh red or green chilli - remove seeds
and finely chop
2 tbsp chopped lemon grass stems (p. 6)
1 tbsp soya sauce
2 tbsp tomato ketchup
4 tbsp black bean sauce (p. 6)
¼ cup water
¼ tsp salt, ¼ tsp pepper, or to taste

METHOD

1 Deep fry tofu or *paneer* till golden brown.

2 String the beans or snow peas. Leave snow peas whole, but cut beans into 2" long pieces. Boil 4 cups water 1 tsp salt and 1 tsp sugar. Add beans or snowpeas to it. Boil for 2 minutes till crisp but tender. Remove from water and refresh in cold water. Keep aside.

3 Heat 3 tbsp oil in a wok, add onions, garlic, ginger, chilli and lemon grass for 2-3 minutes or till onions turn light golden.

4 Add the snowpeas/beans, stir fry for 1-2 minutes. Add the remaining ingredients. Mix well.

5 At serving time, add fried tofu, heat for a minute, serve.

Shrimps/Prawns in Lemon Sauce

Serves 4

INGREDIENTS

8 large shrimps/prawns with tails intact
½ tsp peppercorns - crushed coarsely
oil for deep-frying

BATTER
2 tbsp plain flour (*maida*)
2 tbsp cornstarch
a pinch of baking powder
1 egg, ½ tsp ginger paste
½ tsp garlic paste
½ tsp salt, ½ tsp pepper
¼ tsp red chilli flakes

SAUCE
6 tbsp honey
1 tbsp butter
7- 8 tbsp fresh lemon juice
2 tsp cornstarch mixed with ½ cup water
1 tsp grated ginger, 2 tsp crushed garlic
1 tsp salt, or to taste
3-4 lemon leaves - whole
1-2 drops of lemon yellow food colouring

OTHER INGREDIENTS
1 green onion - only the greens sliced

METHOD

1. Mix all ingredients for the batter. Add 1-2 tbsp water if required to get a thin batter of coating consistency. Keep aside.

2. Heat oil in a wok for deep-frying. Reduce heat. Dip shrimps/prawns, holding the tails, in batter. Do not let the batter coat the tail portion. Drop the shrimps/prawns in oil. Fry on medium heat for just 2-3 minutes till light golden. Do not fry further as the shrimps/prawns will become hard and chewy with overcooking. Remove from oil and keep aside.

3. To prepare the sauce, combine all the ingredients of the sauce, in a pan. Boil the sauce, stirring continuously. Simmer for about 5 minutes till the sauce turns slightly thick and starts to coat the spoon. Remove from heat. Add 1-2 tsp sugar if too sour. Mix. Keep sauce aside.

4. Arrange some greens of onion in a serving platter. Place the fried shrimps/prawns on top.

5. Heat sauce and pour on top of the shrimps/prawns. Serve hot sprinkled with crushed peppercorns.

Stir-Fried Chicken with Cashewnuts

Serves 4

INGREDIENTS

250 g/8 oz boneless chicken - cut into small strips
6-8 mushrooms - cut each in half
2 tbsp oil, 1 tbsp chopped garlic
1 tbsp chopped ginger
1 green onion - cut bulb into 4 pieces & green part into 1" long pieces
½ tsp salt, ½ tsp crushed peppercorns
½ tsp sugar
1 tbsp fish sauce
½ - 1 tbsp soya sauce
½ green and ½ red bell pepper - cut into 1" squares
½ cup roasted or fried cashewnuts
4 fresh red chillies - cut lengthwise

METHOD

1 Heat oil in a frying pan/wok. Fry garlic & white part of onion till onion turns light golden. Add ginger. Stir.

2 Add chicken and mushrooms. Add salt and freshly ground pepper. Fry for 4-5 minutes on medium heat till chicken turns tender.

3 Reduce heat. Add sugar, fish sauce, soya sauce, green and red bell peppers, cashewnuts and red chillies. Saute for 1-2 minutes. Serve hot.

Noodles & Rice

Pineapple Sausage Fried Rice

This dish is very festive to look at. Served in a pineapple shell, it is sure to be a hit. Use a ripe pineapple so that the flesh can be scooped out easily.

Serves 5-6

INGREDIENTS

1½ cups long-grain rice - (boiled 3 cups)
1 ripe pineapple
200 g/6 oz sausages - stir fried & cut into small pieces
100 g/4 oz shrimps, small
3 tbsp butter
1 tsp red chilli paste or red chilli powder
½ tsp garlic paste
1 onion - chopped (½ cup)
¼ cup boiled peas
½ cup coconut milk
3-4 green chillies - chopped
1 tomato - chopped
2-3 tbsp raisins *(kishmish)*
10-12 roasted cashewnuts
2 green onions - chopped along with the green part
2 tbsp fish sauce
1 tbsp soya sauce
1 tsp salt (adjust to taste), 1 tsp pepper
10-15 mint or basil leaves

METHOD

1. Boil 8-10 cups water with juice of 1 lemon and 2 tsp salt. Add rice to boiling water. Boil rice for 7-8 minutes or till done. Strain. Leave in the strainer for 5 minutes for all the water to drain out. Spread out in a large tray to cool.

2. Cut a thin slice of pineapple lengthwise from the top, keeping the leaves on. Scoop out the flesh to create a hollow, with only a thin layer of flesh attached to the inside of the shell. Chop half the flesh into small pieces. (Freeze the other half for future use).

3. Fry sausages, cut into small pieces.

4. Heat butter. Add red chilli paste or powder. Fry for a few seconds.

5. Add garlic and onions. Stir for 2 minutes till onions turn soft.

6. Add coconut milk, shrimps and peas. Cook for 2-3 minutes till shrimps are done.

7. Add all the remaining ingredients. Add the chopped pineapple also. Mix well.

8. Add rice and stir gently till rice is well heated.

9. Warm the pineapple shell in a microwave. Spoon rice into the warmed pineapple shell. Garnish with mint/basil leaves and serve. Alternately, after adding rice, do not heat rice. Spoon into the pineapple shell, cover with aluminium foil and bake in an oven to heat the rice as well as the shell.

Pad Thai

This international favourite has vegetables mixed with sweet and sour flat rice noodles.

Serves 4-5

INGREDIENTS

400 g/12 oz flat rice sticks (noodles)
2 carrots - cut into diagonal slices and
then into strips of ¼" thickness
1 cup bean sprouts with long shoots
(optional)
1 stalk lemon grass - very finely chopped
6-8 lemon leaves - shredded
10 -12 garlic flakes - crushed (1½ tbsp)
1 onion - shredded or thinly sliced
2 tsp salt
1 tsp soya sauce
6-7 tbsp lemon juice
4 tbsp roasted peanuts - coarsely ground
5 tbsp oil

SUGAR SYRUP
3 tbsp sugar mixed with ¼ cup water and
boiled for a minute

RED CHILLI PASTE
4-5 dry red chillies - deseeded and ground
to a paste with 1 tbsp water

METHOD

1 Boil 8-10 cups water with 2 tsp salt and 1 tbsp oil. Add noodles to boiling water. Boil for 2 minutes. Remove from heat. Cover the noodles and let them be in hot water for about 5 minutes or till soft. Strain. Rinse in cold water. Drain and keep aside in the strainer for all the water to drain out. Sprinkle 1 tbsp oil on the noodles and spread in a tray.

2 Prepare sugar syrup and keep aside.

3 Wash sprouts in several changes of water. Leave in the strainer.

4 Heat 5 tbsp oil in a non stick wok or pan. Reduce heat. Add garlic. Stir. Add red chilli paste. Fry for about 1 minute.

5 Add lemon grass, onions and bean sprouts. Fry for 2 minutes till onions turn soft.

6 Add carrots and lemon leaves. Mix. Stir fry for 2 minutes. Reduce heat.

7 Add noodles. Do not mix. Add 2 tsp salt, sugar syrup, lemon juice, soya sauce and 4 tbsp peanuts. Increase heat and mix well using two spoons.

8 Serve hot sprinkled with some roasted and crushed peanuts.

Desserts

Date Pancakes

Serves 8

INGREDIENTS

½ cup cornstarch
½ cup plain flour (*maida*)
¼ cup milk or slightly more
2 tsp melted butter
2 tbsp powdered sugar

FILLING
250 g/8 oz dates- deseeded and finely
chopped (1 cup)
2 tbsp sesame seeds (*til*)
2 tbsp butter, ½ cup water

TO SERVE
vanilla or strawberry ice-cream
some desiccated coconut

METHOD

1   Sift the cornstarch and plain flour together. Add butter and sugar. Add just enough milk and knead to a firm, smooth dough. Cover and keep aside for 15 minutes.

2   For the filling, toast sesame seeds in a non stick pan/skillet till golden. Remove from pan and keep aside. In the same pan melt butter. Add dates and stir for 2 minutes. Add water and cook on low heat for about 2-3 minutes, till a little pulpy and slightly dry. Remove from heat and mix in the toasted sesame seeds. Keep filling aside.

3   Make 8 small balls from the dough. Roll out each ball to a thin chappati.

4   Spread some filling on half of it. Dot the edges with water all around. Fold over to get a semi circle. Press the edges to stick together. Make all pancakes in the same way. Dust them with cornstarch and keep covered with a cling wrap till serving time.

5   To serve, heat a cup of oil in a frying pan and gently slide the stuffed pancake. Shallow-fry on medium heat until crisp, turning sides. Cut into two pieces and top with desiccated coconut. Serve with vanilla ice cream.

GLOSSARY OF NAMES/TERMS

Al' dente	Noodles and vegetables should be cooked to a texture that is not too soft; it should be 'firm to bite' which in Italian is 'al dente'.
Basil	A fragrant herb
Baste	To brush food with fat to prevent it from drying out.
Bean Curd	See tofu
Blanch	To remove skin by dipping into hot water for a couple of minutes. e.g. to blanch tomatoes or almonds.
Blend	To combine two or more ingredients.
Bell Pepper	Capsicum
Cilantro	See coriander
Coriander, fresh	A green herb. All parts of the plant are flavourful and hence edible - leaves, stalks and the Thai also use the root of coriander. Also called cilantro in the west.
Cornflour	Cornstarch
Cream	Whipping cream
Chutney, (mango)	Condiment of fruit, vinegar and spices
Dice	To cut into small neat cubes.
Dough	A mixture of flour, liquid etc., kneaded together into a stiff paste or roll.
Drain	To remove liquid from food.
Garnish	To decorate.
Fish Sauce	A fermented sauce prepared from small fish
Green Onion	Spring onions, scallions
Galangal	Thai ginger
Green Beans	Also called French beans. The tender variety should be used.
Juliennes	To cut into thin long pieces, like match sticks.
Kaffir Lime	A variety of lime found in Thailand
Lemon Grass	Imparts a lemony flavour to the food
Marinate	To soak food in a mixture for some time so that the flavour of the mixture penetrates into the food.
Paneer	The Indian cheese prepared from milk.
Plain Flour	All purpose flour, *maida*.
Red Chilli Powder	Cayenne pepper
Rind	The outer skin of citrous fruits like lemon, orange etc.
Saute	To toss and make light brown in shallow fat.
Shred	To cut into thin, long pieces.
Sift	To pass dry ingredients through a fine sieve.
Snow Peas	The whole flat green pods are edible; the peas are not fully formed.
Star Anise	A star-shaped, fennel-flavoured fruit, dried and used as a spice.
Tofu	Cheese prepared from soya bean milk. Also called bean curd.
Turmeric	A yellow spice with antiseptic properties. Usually available as a powder. It imparts a yellow colour to food.
Toss	To lightly mix ingredients without mashing them e.g. salads.